MY LOVEY DUBEY 2019

STORY FROM YOU AND ME TO US

NISHA MISHRA

ISBN 979-888555637-8

So, i'm dedicating this book to very special person who is so close to me. He is as close as my father mother are in my life. The only man after my father he is. I will say his name Digvijay Singh Rajput. he is the person who taught me the real value of love. He is the only man in my life who changed my life and my thoughts from earlier to now very differently. My book writing is an passion and hobby as well but this first book i ever wanted to write my first book for that particular person who is so close to me. The person who got closer without my permission and became the best part of mine. Thia book is a journey from you and me to us.

He became the reason of publishing this book so soon. I have started writing in 25th of December and after then when i told him about this book. He took so seriously and told me to write in a week. SO, here is our story in a book.

Contents

Foreword vii

Preface ix

Acknowledgements xi

Introduction xiii

Prologue xv

1. August Meeting 1
2. September Function 3
3. October Ups And Downs 16
4. November Glances 19
5. December Love Shower 33

Love Is A Great Feeling 39

Beginning Of Series 2 41

Foreword

MY LOVEY DUBEY Part-1 is a book which is defining love. This book is for all those youngsters who fell in love especially in college. This is a story of Nisha Mishra and Digvijay Singh Rajput named two students of college who fell in love. If you read this book you will start believing in true love or I can say love at first sight. Author and Co author tried to mention all the positive sides of their life. so, people will understand the meaning of love. They put lots of effort in writing this book. Every person who loves reading should read this book. You will get in love with this fantastic and amazing story. The real love life story will make significant mark on your life.

This book encourages positivity and also reliable. The main Aim of this book is to spread their love story and to make people understand. How beautiful love is.

We strongly recommend readers to buy this book. Because it happens sometimes when people share their own experiences from their life.

Foreword

MY LOVELY LORD is a book which is defining love. This book is for all those youngsters who fell in love [illegible]

Preface

MY LOVEY DUBEY 2019 PART-1 It has been written on the bases of two person fell in love. Author decided to take this topic because she wanted to tell their love story all aorund the world. Author gave their time, energy and love to this book. She has been decided to make this book amazing and with no vulgarity. As it is on love life so many of youngsters will buy this book after knowing this amazing story inside the book.

Author took this title of the book from her very childish nature. She mentions her childish behaviour is liked by her partner so she took this name.

Authors also tells us she took just 7 days to write this book. As she was in a challenge to write this book in a week. She tells her pertner announced this book publishing date. So she wrote this book in a specific time. It was her challenging days but she was supported by her partner via phone call.

She also mentions how she took just few days to complete this book whereas she wrote 2,000 words from so long.

Acknowledgements

MY LOVEY DUBEY 2019 PART-1 is a book containing all the information about two person's love. All the information provided in this book is real. I tried to make this book positive in all way. Each chapter of this book is a journey of two people. By each step they grew their love like sowind a seed and growing a tree.

I thank all the characters involved in this to make this book specail and real. As it is the real life book of two people fell in love.

Special thanks to NOTION PRESS to providing me a superb plateform where i get a chance to publish my story as a book.

A big thanks to my Love and Co-author of this book Digvijay Singh Rajput. He helped me to find out all the mistakes and to include all the necessary points of the story.

All the characters in this book deserves thanks because they have done a good job by co-operating.

Introduction

Hey people you are now meeting an author of this book. **Nisha Mishra** born on 22 august,1998 in uttar pradesh. She grew up in the arm of her parents. She mostly travelled northern part of india as her father was in army. She is bold personality who always stood for her and others good rights. She is a girl who loves to interact people but never explored new things alone.

Here you are reaching to Mister Co- author of this book. **Digvijay Singh Rajput** born on 30 august,1997. He grown up with pampered surroundings. He is very innocent person who loves to be good and transparent. He hates who pretend theirself trustworthy but in reality they are not. He belives in family goals. He brung his passion into his career now he owns his gym. He believed in him and he is here.

All the characters including Himanshi, Kamakshi, Shan, Akash brother, Sumit, Digvijay Singh Rajput (co-autor) and Nisha Mishra (author) helped us by including in our story to make it compelete. I specially thank to all.

Prologue

"we can say any one I love You", He said. "According to me it is not for anyone" I told him.He asked me what is the maning of love as your thinking. I told him i know the feeling of love which is so amazing . when you get into this you feel you are in the heaven. I asked the same to him, "What is Love for you"?. He said love is nothing you can say anyone i love you. there is no limitations os saying I Love You. wherever and whenever and whomever you can say this. I told him i usually don't use for anyone. I say I Love You to thsat perso From that day we exchanged our numbers.

He called me by "kattapa" name but I refused to accept this name. I've said "why kattapa". I call everyone with this name so I gave you this name, he said. I told him, "you call Kattapa everyone don't call me with common name. Give me some different name and he said, "Devsina". From that day he started calling me "Devsina". It is some kind of different feeling when you get some different position from others; it's like unique feeling from others. One day I was left alone in my class because of my practical.

CHAPTER ONE

AUGUST MEETING

I anyhow reached in my 2nd year of college and I'm so happy. Because no one knows I've got failed in two of my exams in first semester in which so important to pass atleast main three subjects. And somehow I've managed and reevaluated my one of subject and got passed. Now I'm gonna begin with my first day of my admission when I came after so long because of my re-evaluation result. I was so excited to visit there again because I love the place where I spend most of time with my friends. I'm wearing black suit, with my new hot look. My new hair cut made me so different from my previous year look. And everyone was eager to meet me too. I have done all the formalities of my admission and now I'm a scholar again in this college. There was a senior guy named "Akash" I asked him to drop me on that way where I've to take bus from because our college was recently shifted at that new place. So, there was lack of houses and facilities too. Akash bro sent another boy to drop me off. One boy came to me and said, "Akash told me to drop you down". I was ready to go with him because I've already seen him with bro. That guy was wearing a black mask and his shirt buttons were I guess just two or three were remain shut rest were taking air inside. I said thanks for doing this help to me. (14th of august,2019).

I came next day college and there were regular classes and every co-mates were like,"Nisha you're looking amazing". My new look was stunning and were making everyone shocked. As 5 September was coming so, college function was deciding to rehearsals. As usual I was going to participate in that. I took part in dance and teacher asked me to come for give an audition. After my classes I've reached in a hall to performance so, I can get a chance to get participate. There were so many contestants for college function. Some of were in singing, speech and some of in dance. I was one of them. And now it was my turn and I performed on "kamariya" song from "stree" and everyone astonished. They were like you are superb we have never seen in college, "Nisha". There was a guy who was just so fascinated with my words and my dance as well. The eye of that guy went onto me. From that day he started noticing me. Next day of college and there was a discussion of which song should be performed on. Then ghoomar song from "Padmavat" movie selected. I started practicing on that particular song. So many participants were practicing together. There was a senior guy named "Shan" who sings so well. After my practice, my work was to go and ask him to sing a song from "kabir singh" movie. And that made my days so good. I will also mention about the guy who always helped me in my rehearsals. I've had a guy who told me to how to perform, and where to give my full energy. And he's so good helped me so much.

CHAPTER TWO

SEPTEMBER FUNCTION

Today is 5th of September, whom we celebrate as "Teacher's day". All the performers are set. Program was going well and now my turn came and I was so excited. The glamorous faces and exciting energy of mine was so supportive to my performance. All the things done and many teachers praised me for my performance. Now turn for cake cutting and it was done after than we all have been set up the environment for our mess. We all girls and boys did "Bhangra" over there. After 2 hours of bhangra mess we made each other to go homes. Boy's shirt was like taken from a washing machine this much wet and my uniform was too. Whatsoever was we've enjoyed that moment so much. And that helping guy Shan's friend was asking me to dance more whenever I was stopped. We all were in a mess like so much enjoyful. It was like we had no tension about family it was just so much enjoyment.

6th of September, I was coming back from my AIR HOSTESS INSTITUTE:- University of Life. I saw that Shan's friend was going from there. And when I reached a stop from where I have to change my transport. I was coming down and that guy Shan was standing over there. I astonished, and asked, "What are you doing both here? And I've seen you *before you're going on that way to that guy". "I was picking Shan for college with me," he replied. I actually shocked to see both of them with this scene that they are standing there. They told me teachers asked them to check newspaper where the college function published. But I knew it was just a trick. They were actually for me to take to college with them. But unfortunately it was not happened because I was not going college due to my parents was leaving home for few days. And it was previously decided so, I didn't get ready for college with them. I asked their names I was not conformed to names. They told me their names and very first time I've got Shan's friend name was, "Digvijay Singh Rajput". I literally told, "You have a big name", How will I remember? He told me call him "Diggu". I asked them to change contact number with me but cleverly I just take their numbers, didn't give mine contact. Whenever I'll be going college I'll call you I told them. "But on that day only I'll be there with you" Digvijay murmured. They left the place and conversation ended.*

NEW CHAPTER

As the days have been passed, we 3 get closer in a friendship. He told me about his pen name casually call by his friends was, "Bahubali". He called me by "kattapa" name but I refused to accept this name. I've said "why kattapa". I call everyone with this name so I gave you this name, he said. I told him, "you call Kattapa everyone don't call me with common name. Give me some different name and he said, "Devsina". From that day he started calling me "Devsina". It is some kind of different feeling when you get some different position from others; it's like unique feeling from others. One day I was left alone in my class because of my practical. My co-mates even left college and I was alone. I had no option calling Diggu instead. I called him to drop me to stop but he was unable to get in contact. But I've got my college bus to drop I sat in the bus. And then he called me back asked me for who I am, I told him for the reason of my call. He told me to get off the bus. I went out and waited for him to come. He came from opposite path; he said I was almost to home. And that made me shocked; I've said then why you came to me? He told me just like that. We were going together home. It was very first time when I had a bike ride with him. I just asked him to leave me to stop but he dropped me home. In the entire rout he made me laugh and was creating nonsense to make me smile more. He was doing silly things and making me so scared. He said I'm gonna kidnap you. He asked me what is the maning of love as your thinking. I told him i know the feeling of love which is so amazing . when you get into this you feel you are in the heaven. I asked the same to him, "What is Love for you"?. He said love is nothing you can say anyone i love you. there is no limitations os saying I Love You. wherever and whenever and whomever you can say this. I told him i usually don't use for anyone. I say I Love You to thsat perso From that day we exchanged our numbers.

And it was turning point guys, I didn't know about our future relationship what today is different from that days. If I ever knew about this change of life I think I would do it so earlier. In this meantime god was creating a strong connection between me and him. And of course we are human and don't know about THY GOD miracles. And even can't predict what is going to happen in the very next moment. From that day Nisha and Digvijay were getting in contact again and again but they

don't know about this connection.

However, everything was going fine. But one thing was weird "Diggu" was meeting me again and again. I've shared these things with my friends too. I did not like to be with him all the time. I was like he's so sticky and I don't like him. One day he asked me to go home with him and Sahil. I said no its fine he was like "dar gayi us din ki ride se" I said of course not so, I got ready to go home with them. Now when I was with them of course Sahil was driving and I was sitting after Digvijay. If I say anything about him till now He cares me lot. That's what I loved the most in him. I have had doubt of being so careful about me can be the reason of something. Entire rout they were just speaking stupid stuff and also making me laugh with their silly jokes. For my own security id told them not to go on that way which I don't know about. They said, "We are kidnapping you" I smiled, "seriously my father is in army he will come with his riffle and you both will be killed" I joked. And after some time we all reached at our homes safely. I was left after Sahil so, Diggu decided to drop me before he went home. He became friend of mine like so close friend who has knowledge of my each and every thing now. Now we started calling each other to know if I and he is coming college or not. Those days I was staying alone at home because my parents were not there. So, one day I took leave from college and I was staying home because I have had to wash clothes. He called me to know am I coming college or not I told him the reason I'm not going college. He started laughing because I used to say him how you can take a leave just for cleaning clutter in home and the same thing happened with me. At that day I was busy but still I had something in my mind, "Is he the next". But after that

day I never think about this because I was standing the place where I can't believe at anybody. On that day after coming back from college he called me and said I'm in your area I asked him so, should I come out?. He said, "Yes come out". He and sahil were there when I reached there with my sweetheart blue Maestro named scooty. They were like staring me and also murmuring something. I smiled at him and said, "Hi" both of them. They replied well and Sahil said, "tu yahi shots pehanti hai". I was wearing black knickers and blue top with glasses. Those glasses were making my face fascinating and impressive as well if I say. Sahil said, "You're looking innocent in this glasses". Digvijay complaint me, "you don't reply me on time". I told him that I get busy whole day so, it is impossible to give reply on time. And trust me friends this line was hurting Digvijay so much because at this moment Sahil teased him so much about me. Sahil to Digvijay, "she is not your type girl; leave her she has another world". But you know guys if you have decided to get something with very high dedication then you definitely get that. And my darling is one of them who don't give up easily. But of course Digvijay is a human who also feel bad and hurts. He met next day of college and he told me the whole story but I also declined of that intension he made in his mind. It was so casual reply of that question that's it. Digvijay always liked my talks with him whenever I say he used to watch me all the times. He told me that he loves when I speak. He wants to hear me when I say I found that word cheesy but he has feeling in his wordings. If I say about him till that day I loved his care and attention that he given me all the time. I think that was the think made me compelled bending towards him. One day he messaged me, "Hi" And number was saved with "Bahubali" name. But I didn't reply because I was so busy and was unable to chat. And let me know I've had no android phone where I can chat from! In the evening I called him and we've talked for just 5 to 10 minutes. And then I cut the call. I was feeling so annoy while I interact with him. In the very first month we didn't talk much. I was not sure if he's good or just me thinking much about him. Now Nisha got some feeling about him but was not sure about that if it is true of just fake. Days gone and Time passed now we are good friends and we have started conversations via texting each other. I have a habit of waking up in early morning and health conscious. I was waking up after his good morning texts and that was the sweetest things. I used to wake up in the early morning with my alarms and now his messages are my alarm. Even if I say I used to get up early so he told me to wake him up at that time. And then dropping good morning text in the early morning to him got my duty. My friends I will tell his supreme quality, whenever I sent meassage him he always available for me. The moment I sent text and reply is there. Because of my family restrictions I did not make calls so much but I used to do text mostly. I was compeletly fascinating with his good qualities. I have had my postpaid sim in which I used to pay bill. I've sent many of texts to him and just because of that my bill was from 232 to 654 for the first time it happened. My message limits are 100 for 28 days and I've sent out of limit. Now I got hobby of daily night talks with him. I think it was strong attraction with him. One night when we were texting each other he missed a word and sentence become so worse. I've got angry and we got a fight which was continued for three days. And after few days I came to college and I had my mathematics exam. When I was in the examination hall writing my paper, Diggu was standing just in front of the door. Because he was watching me continuously so, I started smiling. And it was continuous till my exam got over. He asked me to pardon him but I was so confused to forgive him. He took my hand and tried to tap a delete button. Which if was tapped my contact number from his phone would be deleted. He said if you're not talking to me then deletes this number, I don't need this. Before I realized anything he moved home. I called him to ask where he is "I'm going my hometown", he replied. I said sorry and he was normal then. Things were sorted! When he came back from home to college the conversations continued.... I was saying to myself why i'm giving this much importance to him. Days were going good and I was loving company of him now. As I've made promise to me not to get heartily connected to anyone so, I was not touched cordially to him. But if I say he was getting closer to me rather than others. My belief of that time was not to get close to anyone before I get my career done. As I was pursuing air hostess course I used to get busy whole day and he was in sports game so he was going through with those practices. After some days college final match was held in jammu university and our team won and of course he won. As usual in the evening texting I congratulated him and asked him for party. So, the very next day he was ready for giving me party of his winnings. On the next day I came to know he is now a gym trainer in some where's gym. Now I have two reasons to take party from him. We have pre decided to get party done after college dispersion. I asked him to wait till dispersion of college. He waited for me but some of my friends were with me I forgot to tell him about I can't come to take party and he kept waiting. When I reached bus stop he called me and asked where I am. I told him I'm in a bus going home. He got angry and of course I made him angry I was the only reason even I should be sorry. I called him back to say sorry but he didn't pick my call so, I waited for next day to sort it up. Next day, I tried to make everything sorted but happened something bad. On the same day my friend who is so close "Sumit" came and he took me to canteen where I had asked to wait for my Bahubali after college dispersion.

When he reached I was already with my friend, I asked him to be seated. Diggu was with his friend Shan. I've got busy with Sumit in talks and walks. In the meantime, Diggu left canteen. I tried to call him back but he didn't pick my call, he dropped me a message, "RAHO BUSY APNE PURANE DOSTON KE SATH.OLD IS GOLD". This was too much. At that time I got confused between these things why he has this jealous and why I'm so conscious about him for his silly angry nature. If he is willing to keep this friendship continue then he will come back. So, with these thoughts I was going with this friendship.

NEW CHAPTER

As the days have been passed, we 3 get closer in a friendship. He told me about his pen name casually call by his friends was, "Bahubali". He called me by "kattapa" name but I refused to accept this name. I've said "why kattapa". I call everyone with this name so I gave you this name, he said. I told him, "you call Kattapa everyone don't call me with common name. Give me some different name and he said, "Devsina". From that day he started calling me "Devsina". It is some kind of different feeling when you get some different position from others; it's like unique feeling from others. One day I was left alone in my class because of my practical. My co-mates even left college and I was alone. I had no option calling Diggu instead. I called him to drop me to stop but he was unable to get in contact. But I've got my college bus to drop I sat in the bus. And then he called me back asked me for who I am, I told him for the reason of my call. He told me to get off the bus. I went out and waited for him to come. He came from opposite path; he said I was almost to home. And that made me shocked; I've said then why you came to me? He told me just like that. We were going together home. It was very first time when I had a bike ride with him. I just asked him to leave me to stop but he dropped me home. In the entire rout he made me laugh and was creating nonsense to make me smile more. He was doing silly things and making me so scared. He said I'm gonna kidnap you. From that day we exchanged our numbers.

And it was turning point guys, I didn't know about our future relationship what today is different from that days. If I ever knew about this change of life I think I would do it so earlier. In this meantime god was creating a strong connection between me and him. And of course we are human and don't know about THY GOD miracles. And even can't predict what is going to happen in the very next moment. From that day Nisha and Digvijay were getting in contact again and again but they don't know about this connection.

However, everything was going fine. But one thing was weird "Diggu" was meeting me again and again. I've shared these things with my friends too. I did not like to be with him all the time. I was like he's so sticky and I don't like him. One day he asked me to go home with him and shan. I said no its fine he was like "dar gayi us din ki ride se" I said of course not so, I got ready to go home with them. Now when I was with them of course shan was driving and I was sitting after Digvijay. If I say anything about him till now He cares me lot. That's what I loved the most in him. I have had doubt of being so careful about me can be the reason of something. Entire rout they were just speaking stupid stuff and also making me laugh with their silly jokes. For my own security id told them not to go on that way which I don't know about. They said, "We are kidnapping you" I smiled, "seriously my father is in army he will come with his riffle and you both will be killed"

I joked. And after some time we all reached at our homes safely. I was left after shan so, Diggu decided to drop me before he went home. He became friend of mine like so close friend who has knowledge of my each and every thing now. Now we started calling each other to know if I and he is coming college or not. Those days I was staying alone at home because my parents were not there. So, one day I took leave from college and I was staying home because I have had to wash clothes. He called me to know am I coming college or not I told him the reason I'm not going college. He started laughing because I used to say him how you can take a leave just for cleaning clutter in home and the same thing happened with me. At that day I was busy but still I had something in my mind, "Is he the next". But after that day I never think about this because I was standing the place where I can't believe at anybody. On that day after coming back from college he called me and said I'm in your area I asked him so, should I come out?. He said, "Yes come out". He and shan were there when I reached there with my sweetheart blue Maestro named scooty. They were like staring me and also murmuring something. I smiled at him and said, "Hi" both of them. They replied well and shan said, "tu yahi shots pehanti hai". I was wearing black knickers and blue top with glasses. Those glasses were making my face fascinating and impressive as well if I say. shan said, "You're looking innocent in this glasses". Digvijay complaint me, "you don't reply me on time". I told him that I get busy whole day so, it is impossible to give reply on time. And trust me friends this line was hurting Digvijay so much because at this moment shan teased him so much about me. shan to Digvijay, "she is not your type girl; leave her she has another world". But you know guys if you have decided to get something with very high dedication then you definitely get that. And my darling is one of them who don't give up easily. But of course Digvijay is a human who also feel bad and hurts. He met next day of college and he told me the whole story but I also declined of that intension he made in his mind. It was so casual reply of that question that's it. Digvijay always liked my talks with him whenever I say he used to watch me all the times. He told me that he loves when I speak. He wants to hear me when I say I found that word cheesy but he has feeling in his wordings. If I say about him till that day I loved his care and attention that he given me all the time. I think that was the think made me compelled bending towards him. One day he messaged me, "Hi" And number was saved with "Bahubali" name. But I didn't reply because I was so busy and was unable to chat. And let me know I've had no android phone where I can chat from! In the evening I called him and we've talked for just 5 to 10 minutes. And then I cut the call. I was feeling so annoy while I interact with him. In the very first month we didn't talk much. I was not sure if he's good or just me thinking much about him. Now Nisha got some feeling about him but was not sure about that if it is true of just fake. Days gone and Two months passed now we are good friends and we have started conversations via texting each other. I have a habit of waking up in early morning and health conscious. I was waking up after his good morning texts and that was the sweetest things. I used to wake up in the early morning with my alarms and now his messages are my alarm. Even if I say I used to get up early so he told me to wake him up at that time. And then dropping good morning text in the early morning to him got my duty. My friends I will tell his supreme quality, whenever I sent meassage him he always available for me. The moment I sent text and reply is there. Because of my family restrictions I did not make calls so much but I used to do text mostly. I was compeletly fascinating with his good qualities. I have had my postpaid sim in which I used to pay bill. I've sent many of texts to him and just because of that my bill was from 232 to 654 for the first time it happened. My message limits are 100 for 28 days and I've sent out of limit. And that bill was paid by him. Now I got hobby of daily night talks with him. I think it was strong attraction with him. One night when we were texting each other he missed a word and sentence become so worse. I've got angry and we got a fight which was continued for three days. And after few days I came to college and I had my mathematics exam. When I was in the examination hall writing my paper, Diggu was standing just in front of the door. Because he was watching me continuously so, I started smiling. And it was continuous till my exam got over. He asked me to pardon him but I was so confused to forgive him. He took my hand and tried to tap a delete button. Which if was tapped my contact number from his phone would be deleted. He said if you're not talking to me then deletes this number, I don't need this. Before I realized anything he moved home. I called him to ask where he is "I'm going my hometown", he replied. I said sorry and he was normal then. Things were sorted! When he came back from home to college the conversations continued.... I was saying to myself why i'm giving this much importance to him. Days were going good and I was loving company of him now. As I've made promise to me not to get heartily connected to anyone so, I was not touched cordially to him. But if I say he was getting closer to me rather than others. My belief of that time was not to get close to anyone before I get my career done. As I was pursuing air hostess course I used to get busy whole day and he was in sports game so he was going through with those practices. After some days college final match was held in jammu university and our team won and of course he won. As usual in the evening texting I congratulated him and asked him for party. So, the very next day he was ready for giving me party of his winnings. On the next day I came to know he is now a gym trainer in some where's gym. Now I have two reasons to take party from him. We have pre decided to get party done after college dispersion. I asked him to wait till dispersion of college. He waited for me but some of my friends were with me I forgot to tell him about I can't come to take party and he kept waiting. When I reached bus stop he called me and asked where I am. I told him I'm in a bus going home. He got angry and of course I made him angry I was the only reason even I should be sorry. I called him back to say sorry but he didn't pick my call so, I waited for next day to sort it up. Next day, I tried to make everything sorted but happened something bad. On the same day my friend who is so close "Sumit" came and he took me to .canteen where I had asked to wait for my Bahubali after college dispersion. When he reached I was already with my friend, I asked him to be seated. Diggu was with his friend Shan. I've got busy with Sumit in talks and walks. In the meantime, Diggu left canteen. I tried to call him back but he didn't pick my call, he dropped me a message, "RAHO BUSY APNE PURANE DOSTON KE SATH.OLD IS GOLD". This was too much. At that time I got confused between these things why he has this jealous and why I'm so conscious about him for his silly angry nature. If he is willing to keep this friendship continue then he will come back. So, with these thoughts I was going with this friendship.

CHAPTER THREE

OCTOBER UPS AND DOWNS

Today is 2nd of October and I have my anchoring in college. I was conducting the whole show with one of my co mate. He helped me in writing my anchoring speech with good handwriting. Friends I'll tell you I have very bad handwriting. I don't write tidy and neat and he is totally opposite. He always was with me in every times doesn't matter if have fought with him or not. He was not interested in sitiing that auditorium but he attended because I was there of course so. He attended just because of that stupid and boring function. We all know nobody wants to hear that so boring speeches and for so long. It was almost 6to 8 speeches I guess was in the queue. He is kind of non politician person and very transparent so he doesn't like fake people in his life. In that auditorium there were jaggu like people whom he doesn't like anyhow. He was not wanted to see all that politic stuff. I don't know why he is so closed to me but it was so good for me. i was loving that care that attention he was providing me. One more quality of him is he has care of mine always. If I have fight with him still he made sure all the times if I left college, if I'm reached home safely. My parents came home and so, I told him I'll go myself. One day he texted me to ask me where I am and I was about to home. He texted me, "Dil tod ke hasti ho mera wafayein meri yaad karogi". My reply on that text was, "Agar jinda rahi tab karungi na yaad". His friend Shan always tries to get in competition with him but he can't as my Darling is different. He has jealousy as well for others. If anyone else does flirt or some try he gets some anger and jealousy as well. Even sometimes my brain got confused is he really getting close to me or just a friend type jealous.. I've decided to talk less but he was like in my mind. We were not in contact for some days. And college had some off days in between we had no contact I thought now that's all. We are going to done mow, whatsoever was going to touch the end. In the off days My institution told me to get done with my hair smoothening. On 21st of October I've done my smoothening and after that I went on college 22nd of October. Everybody was complimenting me but I was searching one person to say sorry and to talk to him. He was peeped but disappeared again like a fume. When I started searching him I found him sitting on a corner seat in a classroom writing something on a page. When I reached closer I found him writing "beast" on a page this much badly the pages under that page would get perfect cut. He was not looking at me so, took his phone started doing silly things. I open up photos gallery. He said I have a movie in which a girl looks just like you. Whenever I see her she reminds me of you. I extremely likening that complimentary. I was eager to know who the girl is he talking about. So, on my request he showed me picture of that girl. My mind was being like "And I know that character already, well she was looking so simple and beautiful too (thank god)". I played music "Dekhte Dekhte" song and I was lip sing with my silly acting. I guess it was irritating him but he was enjoying actually. I complained about no compliment from him for my smoothening. My words were like "nobody complimented on so spent expenses smoothened hair". He smiled and said "bilkul nahi ache lag rhe". I was like seriously! My mind was fucked up. He really saying I'm not looking good in this. After that I was refused to say I'm looking good enough. But he said "you're looking beautiful". But I like your curly hair. You look like Alena'D curlz from "Rustom" movie in that short curly hair. Seriously I was blushed at that time. I've realized he like me in that way. But one thing I always noticed in him is he does care of mine. I think this was the reason I changed my thought for being in a relationship. This was the thing bending me towards him. After accepting my sorry we have decided to have party in alone after college. We went to canteen we sat in front of each other, now we are so free. We had order something to eat. And that's how our day was spent. Now he always used to pick and drop from home. We have started going together and also I begin waiting at Mishriwala to let him pick me up to college. And this is how we have decided to do for so long. And we didn't know about what is going on in our life. But this time one person was aware of all these things and he was none other than Digvijay. He fell in love with me at first sight but never told me. Things were going very casualy and Nisha was completely unknown with the things were happening around him. It was Digvijay who was so careful about relationship doesn't whatsoever it was. He always made sure to make this feeling and connection stronger but there was me who only fought with him at very silly things. My October month almost went fully with these ups and downs for my relationship with him. One thing I will definitely mention he has hate of my friends specially one whose name is Sumit. He hates him because he was so close friend of mine. He has habit of hugging me whenever he meets me and not even him but Sumit doesn't like him too. If I actually say the perfect word for them is conflicts between two (chattis ka aakda).

CHAPTER FOUR

NOVEMBER GLANCES

November starts and our relationship is at high glances. We never accepted it as our couples but we did like that. In the while I got some update from my institution I have to go Delhi. So for that I have do lots of preparation like my uniform and photographs and lot more. I had to do it alone but no I was not alone. One person was there who was helping me so much. Now today is Sunday and I'm going market to shop my formals. I was with my mom and sister. We were already messaging each other. And I told him about my shopping. I went Apsara at Gandhinagar in Jammu. The twist point of this timing was he messaged me, "where I am" I was shocked because I already told him. He told me I'm in gole market. "In which transport you are" he asked. I surprisingly asked him if he is here. And yeah he was there for me. Anyhow I realized he might be here around me because he texted me you are wearing white top right? It was so surprise for me I was continuously smiling he was in my same bus. And my smile was continuing till he got down the bus. He was with Shan they both were together just for me. It was the first time he travelled in public transport he never did this before. For me he travelled just to see me. I don't know what it was but something. I had no idea about the things were going with me. Either it was love or some kind of attraction. It was it with my shopping. On the next day we met in college and I said why you came there silly. He said Shan had some work and he asked me to go with him so I came there. But friends this was not logically correct right? I know. As our party was pending so he told me to go with him there in canteen. I and he went restaurant named Hot and Cold café. We sat there when he has no money. He said, "I have no money" but I ignored and here we are. After a while we ordered something to eat and he had nothing except 20 rupees. And 20 rupees note is still with me as a token of our first date. He said our first date is like we have nothing it is with no money. First date and with no money. We even laugh today if we recall that moment. We have ordered Momos to eat because at that time we two were on diet for so long. He told me about how bad happened with him in the past and I also shared the things of my past life. He is funny he said "he is a serial kisser". I laughed at her and said "I'm not a serial kisser but I do intensively when I'm with my partner, I'm kind of romantic person who don't compromises with time lackness just go with romances. He just settled my words in his mind. But the first date with him was so funny but memorable too for life long. Next day I was staying home because I have had some work to do. And he reached college alone of course he was missing me so much. It is very obvious when you get interact any new person in your life you got habit of that individual and it's not wrong. I think it was happening with him so, it was something like with him. He messaged me, "payment done" and it is for that date. Because we had no money we took debt of rupees something to eat Momos and that payment was done today. Finally, it was successful date with no money and lots of talks. We I think were in a confusion of our relationship in between us at that time. One day after dispersion we were sitting together in the canteen and were just having serious talks about future. He begun with such no *sense talks like, "you have so much fan following can I be the one of them". I literally laughed and said, "Seriously, yeah you can be 50th of them in a queue". It was seriously stupid talking trust me. He actually asked if we can be together in future!. I told him it's just not only you and not just about you but for anyone because if I get settled I can have my own choice. I can select my partner by my own. He was really smiling and said, "matlab meri baat ban sakti hai". I said yeah of course yrr. I think that day changed his second thoughts about me. That day was like a step towards our relationship. He was already in love with me but was not just sharing me because we already have been discussed about past things and not be in relationship. I and he were so sure about our strong bond in this relation. I had to click photographs for my interview was going held in Delhi. I and my friends have decided to meet at one of my friend's home. He took me to that place where I have had to click photographs I was carrying my formals and we all have to gather in a city. He droped me at point of place and he was leaving the place but I stopped him and introduced him with all of my friends. The moment he left my friends started teasing me with his name and by his company with me. They were insisting me to get in a relationship with him. I was saying nothing just smiling I guess it was if I say blush on my cheeks for no reason. These days were like I and darling were getting closer. One day it was raining and very romantic weather it was. He took me at "sai restaurant" to have some personal time. There were no rush and just me and he was there. I think I was bit nervous though it was not a girlfriend and boyfriend type date but the nervousness was just like that. He ordered something to eat and ordered coffee for me. As he knew I love coffee and chocolates. I'm gonna share the things happen there while sitting there. He was sitting in front of me I asked him to sit next to me, so I can comfortably talk to him* *and the moment I told him to sit over there he smiled so much. We have shared lots of things to each other also discussed about career and marriages. There we have decided to get in a perfect bond and to knowing each other very well. If everything will be fine we will get married. And from that day we have started to notice and observe each other for future relationship we had no idea what will happen in future but we have decided to start knowing each other and to give time each other of ourselves. The story of getting closer has begun from that day. I remember when we were sitting at that restaurant his friends were calling him again and again to know what is happening there. But it was nothing like that they were thinking might be we are having kisses or hugs like other couples do. We made confirmation about ourselves. Now we have started knowing each other very well. We talked about our culture differences as I'm from Lucknow and he is from Jammu. So, it's obvious we have different cultures and different environment. It was so important to know each other very well. I told him about my family members and he told me about his family members. I discussed how my father owned everything by his own hard work and he told me too about his hard work father. The day I have started being with him his female friends were jealous with me I don't know why. There was a girl the same name of mine she was so jealous to me. And it was completely different and weird too for me. Here I'm gonna share very interesting part of us was he liked in me is my way of talking to everyone with huge respect. And I liked him by his good nature and because of his comfortable, flexible zone. He was from one day so comfortable for me. I and darling are the person who did not used even a single bad word for each other. I think god has created and made us for each other. I and he were used to be together whole day till 4'o clock. And this much is enough to know anyone. The days were coming close of my interview.*

My screening was going to held in Delhi at Gurgaon 16th of November, I had to go there so before that my grooming should be done. And for that I had to take leave from college for my holidays. I came to college to take leave. And I also wanted to let him know about this so, I went there to let him know about this. And he was in library I told him about my screening and he told me about externals he is practicing about. We had time alone in canteen discussed so many things with each other. On 13th of November when we were coming back from college he took me to a cosmetic shop to buy some of my facial cosmetics for interview makeup. Today I didn't go college so that I can get done my grooming before my interview. 15th of November 7:45 in the evening we had to leave homes to institute. We all have had to gather over there before going in a bus. I'm in the bus and he is texting me continuously and I'm with my di. When I, Di and Himanshi met at jeewal, he was also there and he came to me and shook my hand I told him to not to say you are my friend, you are Himanshi's friend instead. Everything was set he texted after leaving from there "I have a chocolate for you but how could I give you so, I didn't give you in front of your sister". My mind was like "seriously chocolate and you didn't give me". Literally my heart was crying for that chocolate. Friends believe me he was in contact till I reached Delhi but also just a friend. We were messaging and updating each step by my side. I was actually confused about our relation but also reminding me all the times he is just my friend. I do not have to forget about I'm focused I can't repeat the mistake happened in my past. But what would you do guys if you are surrounded with free and very good deal, "Won't you grab that"? Of course yes. I've reached Delhi with our girl gang. Very first time my experience in metro. I liked traveling from Jammu to Delhi. But I've also realized nothing in this world like home. All the times he was in contact till my interview done.

He sent me messages for my best wishes I read all of them but after my interview because there was hush and rush for interview timing so we were getting late for that. From PG to Location we travelled alone. And we had no idea about where to go and how. Just spend money and then only you can go. We girl gang were roaming here and there after interview. We got nothing just a gol gappe wali stall and went there to stop out mouth water. We spent our day with so much fun. We danced, with no loud music and no restrictions. We had lots of enjoyment Himanshi was wearing just sleeveless top and knickers and many of girls were making mess. The moment was so cool I was enjoying with lots of fun. Kamakshi was the girl who just spent her whole time on phone call and on messages too. Because I have had my sim which was working so she took that for chating with her boyfriend. When she slept the phone was beeping and yeah it was her messages from her boyfriend, it was "love you babu", "good nini". I have read all the messages I know this is wrong but it was my phone with typing keypad so no lock was available so she can hide or I can ignore any one message. It was fully enjoying for me. My sister and friends were so crazy they have ordered zomato at late night. It was like 12:45 when she has ordered pizza to eat. That's how we spent that day and in the next morning we were arranging morning breakfast for 6 of our group. I and himanshi went out to get breakfast with us. As usual I called him and we were talking at that time I have stopped call waiting services that's why whenever people tries to call me they hears busy tune. So, while ongoing call my sister called me too and happen the same. She was so angry because she made atleast 20 to 25 calls. We have reached PG and happened fight between us two. I was just waiting for the time to come back home. Because whatsoever you can have outside but the food and relaxation you are provided at your home can't get outside.

After two days in Delhi I came back home but I have bought a watch for him. It was worth rupees 100 not more than that. I thought might be he will like it. He got to know about I'm coming back to jammu. After coming back I've messaged him that I'm home. He was having his 5th semester exams at that time. He texted me I'm in your area and I used to come out to see him. Just silly things to share with you but I did that with so much interest. May be guys you will found this so much cheesy but it is truth and it happened actually. I gave him watch when I came to college with him. Even I asked him to wear that watch. He was happy with that such cheap gift I bought for him. It was for him like a diamond he was taking care of that watch. He has fond of qualities I have not so much words to say. I found I'm distracting from my track I think so I've decided just ignore him. I was ignoring his calls and messages. He was calling me continuously so picked that up and said, "don't call me and don't text me". I don't want my focused life ruined and with these last words I cut the call. It was rude but I was chaos between him and my future. I thought he is a barrier in my career life. My focus for my career was disturbed because he entered in my life I think I got conscious about my future. This entire conversation was held when I was coming back from my institute. On very next day he met me and trying to handover my watch to me but I refused to take it back that thing which I gave already to someone. "It is gifted to you how I can take it back" I shouted. He is always polite he told me if you don't want to talk to me then why your things will be with me take it. My life was totally confused because I was stuck. In this fight there was a scene created I don't remember actually it was I or He thrown watch down the floor. At the moment watch fell down it smashed and the subtle pieces of watch frame was spread all around the corridor. This was so worse than anything. I was so ashamed on that work done by *me. It was huge mistake I made I was so regretting myself. I didn't do that. My heart was screaming why I have done this because I have never been this munch angry I mean I don't harm anything in my aggression. I'm not that type of girl but I did that. It was worst day of mine in college. I was going my institute and that thoughts were coming in my mind. I message him, "tell me how much you have spent on me I will return you". I think it was silly message and funny as well but trust me I sent him this text. He called me at the moment and said, "Give me my money back it is more than 7000 rupees". He asked me to come at that right time to give his money back and he was laughing. That anger turned into funny moment within a second. Each words coming from side was made him laughing. After a while of conversation we got back to normal conversation. Next day in college he told me when I threw watch over the floor, he tried to recollect pieces but after a while he thrown not just those pieces but his own watches too. What he was wearing from so long. I was guilty but it can't be undone.*

He always made mark on my fights with token of love. He is like a kiss on a deep wound. He always had a calm and polite reaction towards my side. I think this is love for me from the beginning of the day. From very first day he proved how lovely he is. He is actually sweetheart so I was falling towards him. Till now if I say I am the only reason of each fight. Each conflict was happened because of me in between us. I am to blame for each fight. As we were on the track of knowing and growing together so, most of the time in college I used to with him. Whenever I get free I went to him. Mostly in college including teachers too were thinking we are in a relationship. In their sight we are girlfriend and boyfriend. Even mostly girls who know me used to call him, "jiju". This is so common in india when two are in a relationship friends of one girl call his boy, "jiju" and friends of that one boy call her girl, "Bhabhi".

Whenever I needed he was with me for my projects which were online. And let me tell you those days were totally offline. At that time internet services was closed. The whole area was without internet services. And because of that so many projects and assignments were done at cyber café. This was the time when we get closer due to this. He always helped me to reach cyber café at Bohri. We started meeting earlier in the morning one hour prior of college classes. We spent most of time in canteen together. That became the sitting spot of ours. He used to order Aloo Paratha, Onion Paratha and cheese paratha. Before meeting him I and Darling were on diet. But when we met we have just killed our diet and cracked limit of eating paratha and chocolates. He used to buy chocolates for me as he knew that I love chocolates so much. He always made my wishes true and obeyed my orders for his safety regards. He is a kind of sweet person who doesn't hurt people. I always have been dying with his fascinating nature. We used to sit at two of places which were canteen nearest to college and that cyber café. It was almost close to December. He has habit of being so close to me like no matter where we are just stand next to me. We used to grip hands in college too. I have said to him that I don't care about this fake world I just have a fear of my parents that's it. We used to spend most of time together alone. We now understand each other enough. We at least give respect and understand I don't have to say this word. I never liked to be disrespected and not to use bad words for anyone. This was the rule what he likes the most. One day in college my computer teacher told me something about how teachers speak about those girls. I don't want you to be the one of them. So, I would recommend not to clutch hands and not to stand together you two. I actually tanked him about this teaching. I told him about this he got anxious and got upset. I asked him not to clutch my hand at least in college. But he had problem with this restriction, he said "does it matters for you because you told me earlier that you don't care about people". I was shocked he is really amazing look at his sharp memory. His memory is like actually he ate so many almonds. I was smiling and said, "But this is my college where I have to study after you too". So, I can't ruin my image here with my own hand. He just left the place not just the place but college at that time. I was running after him for asking to stay but, He gone. I was going alone in transport he called me and said how you going and where you are. I told him don't ask if you left me alone there. I am okay and going cyber café I have some work over there. He said okay come then. I was thinking about his last words because I was confused if he said go then or come then. There I got my friends call and she told me he is waiting over there. I smiled and thought he can't change himself no matter how much we have fought; He always took care of mine. I reached over the place and I shook my hand with my friend. Avoiding him and going straight he asked me to stop I will drop you there. But I didn't hear I was going straight, he stood his bike just beside to me. After all I had to sit on his bike because I didn't want show any drama in public. I sat and told him to drop me before the place. When I was sitting in cyber café he came after me over there and sat just next to me. I was smiling though he was upset because of this nonsense thing. So, I told him not to worry about these shit things we will not take that seriously. Things which will come in between a relationship, things which can create lot of misunderstanding between two can't be good. I did what I was doing regularly. We came next day and with clutched hands I was just waiting for the day when any of teachers will say to me anything. Even many times people living in my area saw me with him but luckily happened nothing. After a week when I was coming back from institute one of my friends told she is hungry but we had no money. So, I had an option of calling Diggu and he said he is coming within a minute. We waited at Kwality Restaurant for him. And here he comes and we entered inside the restaurant and ordered something to eat. As Himanshi loves Dosa so she ordered that and I have ordered noodles because I love that. Diggu ordered "Naan" for him and we have started talking. I introduced him with Himanshi and Himanshi was introduced with him. We have done with the introduction and he smiled while he was sitting next to my seat. Himanshi was crazy she said, "You both looking nice together". I was like shut up we are just friends c'mon. My heart was flying I guess don't know why but I was smiling when she said this. Himanshi and Diggu had conversations about me. He was praising me and she was telling him about me. They both were discussing how I am. I remember Himanshi said to him, "You are so lucky otherwise Nisha don't allow people to come in her life this much closer especially boys and also you are lucky sitting beside her because she slaps boys". He laughed and stared at me and said, "She is lioness". Well you look actually good together, you should get in a relationship, Himanshi insisted. I was flushing at that moment and it was my sister's call who was calling me from so long to know where I am because she has doubt where I can be. We had finished our dishes and moved from restaurant to home. But before that we took selfie. As I have mentioned I had no android phone at that time, Himanshi asked Diggu to take his phone out. His phone was old from Lava brand. He refused to click picture from his phone. There after no option left except Himanshi's phone. We took selfie and moved home. *I Himanshi and Diggu were on his bike named "Avenger". He dropped me at my stop after Himanshi. It was enjoying day till I was with him. He was so warm in that chilled winter. I have lots of memories with him he made each moment memorable with his care, respect and attention.*

In college after being with him so many dramas happened like sometimes his friends had problems and sometimes mine had. Sometimes seniors got some nonsense acting towards him. One day when college was in inspection days it was announced no student will allowed without full uniform. As a senior I had this duty to maintain the discipline of college and I did it. There was a girl wearing pink jacket and with no dupatta. I told her to take dupatta from tomorrow and also wear college sweater it was happened in the morning and in the afternoon around 1'o clock a boy came to me and said, "why you told that girl to wear this and not that. Blah blah". I was surprised and asked him, "what is he all talking about". He told me about that pink jacket girl and I replied on that with very reaction. He warned me not to say her anything. That was so rude and nonsense, "I will stop everyone who is not following discipline and that's my duty,I will do no one can stop me alright!" I shouted. While shouting at him Diggu comes and asking me what happened who was he what he is saying to you and all. He was concerned for me and wanted to know so, he pulled my hand to know the thing happened there. akash came there to make just a significant mark on college people. He is just nonsense guy in the whole college. He just started shouting at him and said, "Why you clutching her hand, this is vulgarity don't spread it please" Don't do it. I was unable to understand what is happening this, even I shouted bro he is not pulling my hand and spreading vulgarity. He just wanted to know what is wrong with me that was it and you made this big issue. Diggu left the place it was so embarrassing for him to hear and bear the entire thing. I left things all I just moved towards him for asking his well being. He told me there was principle with other staff so he was shouting and I didn't shouted at him back because I was not in uniform. He went outside college and waited for me till dispersion of college. I never wanted him to feel hurt because of me but it was not a single day when he is not get upset and insulted just because of me no matter how much. This happened so wrong to him.

In the evening when I was going institute he called me and said, "I've got new phone". He told me he did his first call to me with new phone. That gave me special feeling I was smiling and I expressed it too. We too are good enough to understand to understand each other's silence. I was kept silent till he asked me what happened. You give me so much importance that's why I like you so much. Your attention makes me overwhelmed. I thank to god you meet me. Conversation ended with saying, "I'll show you my phone next day in college.

Next day he came in uniform after 12'o clock. It was kind of bang entry of a hero. He comes and I saw him from first floor I ran down to him I shook hand and hugged him. It was relaxed zone for me. Although I never felt him something else except a friend. But I also have feeling more than a friend. He was getting closer day by day. He was making an impact into my heart. It was like something miracle happening to me. I never took him so seriously about our love relationship but there was something which was keep going between us and was very different. He bought new phone latest trending brand "Real me". He showed me his phone. It was a special feeling when he clutched my hand in front of students and said, "Let see who speaks shit about us". We two have our rule from the very first day is, "we are, and we will be together". I was satisfying myself he had a new phone now. I took his phone till the dispersion time. One thing what I liked in between our bond is we never asked each other for anything. We trusted each other always we never did cheap things like restricting each other for stupid things. But it was true he felt jealousy so many times when I stand with my male friends. I don't know why girls never feel jealous why just boys? I was so smiling by taking his phone in my hand. I was roaming all around the college with him. He handed over his phone to me for all the times. After dispersion I clicked photo when he was driving bike. And it was first picture I have clicked in his phone. He still has those photographs. I was enjoying my picture clicking session because the picture quality of that camera was so good. It so good time when I clicked some of pictures. November was like I like him so much. I was engaged with the habbit of his attention and his respect for me. His lovely behaviour was changing my perspective for boys and for love. His treatment for me was like pampering a baby. His most of time was for me only, we used to sit on side table in the canteen. Where we ate momos , stuffed parathan and lots of chocolates. His respect for me and giving me lot of importance compelled me to get close to him. with the ending of November I got so close to him.

CHAPTER FIVE

DECEMBER LOVE SHOWER

Today is 5th of December and I have received my phone bill through message of rupees 636. After this message I got call and it was from him. He asked me to get ready for college and meet me on 08:15 at your stop. I've got ready and was reaching to my stop before I reached stop he reached behind me and was blowing horn with the sound, "pee pee pee". I told him about my bill that my bill reached this much. How will I pay, he smiled and said as usual I will pay don't worry. He is not my just partner but also solution of my each question. He always there for me whenever I got need. Unluckily, I never have to him when he needed me. Well, he never got that circumstance where I had to help him. I was with him in his classroom and we were just sitting together. Teacher comes and asked us what we are doing here very aggressively. I might be getting quiet if she asked with politely but she was rude with us. Despite of leaving the room I asked her back, "can't we sit here?" He holds my hand asked me to be quiet and not to say anything. I was angry on that teacher because I didn't like her behavior of being rude to us. I felt good to leave that classroom else, I would definitely shout on her. Teachers have their own negative thoughts about a girl and boys being together. This is the thing I will mention here teachers should change their opinion about a girl and a boy when they are together. I have seen so many times during my studies weather in school or in college teachers always point that girl who comes in contact with boys. But also they mention co-education is good parents should not think negative about it.

December is a new step in our love life. Digvijay paid my bill in the evening. And I got a message of my paid bill. Nisha got feeling for Digvijay. One thing was there which was stopping her to not get into love. Her past was so bad about love. She was worried if past will repeat itself then what she will do. She was confused but also accepting Digvijay lovely nature he can't cheat on her. One thing in between them was they have shared each and everything each other. When she got this confusion she talked to him and here is some conversation.

"What is the proof you will never leave me" I frowned.

"If you don't trust me no issue but I just can say I want to marry you" he replied.

"Everyone says the same word, may be you are just impressing me" I asked.

"May be you are right but what about my feelings, you are mature enough to read my feelings" he told.

"okay than let me think" I smiled and said.

We two had lots of conversations and understood now what to do. But after that conversation I've got to know about his feelings for me. He loves me lot and I don't know about me. I was confused to just express infront of him but deep down I was feeling something special for him.

One day I and he were sitting in a canteen and he was saying that he said I will tell you how to keep a gap while sharing chocolate from lip to lip. It was weird but I did. You won't believe but I was so flushed after doing this. He took a piece of chocolate and griped into teeth and asked me to cut it from but without touching lips. It was happened with lots of my energy and effort from inside. After this I was like nothing happened. Mean while we were noticed the hit in our hearts. My heart beat was so faster when it happened. He told me he loves my childish behavior, he loves how I give respect him; he loves my talking way which is so polite. I told him about his goodness how he is special for me. I told him the thing I like in him the most is his care and attention towards me.

One day I was sitting with my friend and he hugged me suddenly tightly. He said I just wanted to so I did it. It was like he is in mood of romantic. I always known for bold in college. Everyone knew I have a dream to have romantic man in my life. One day he came because I was alone in college and I had my practical in college. He was not coming because it was raining and he came for me. It was my mistake I was standing with my friends and he had to wait for me for so long. Again he got upset because of me but I controlled situation by saying sorry. December rides on his bike with him were like a warm blanket in chilled winter. He and I used to play songs while he driving. Here are some of favorite songs: - Yaad piya ki ane lagi, Kinna sona, Chosen, etc. I will explain whole scenario of having warm ride sitting behind him every day was like a great energy in me developing. He used to set mirror of his bike to see me perfectly and when sees me I feel blushed. Till the end of song he lip sing and watches me all the times.

When everything was fine and we were getting in a perfect bond. Then one day his friends asked us to play truth and dare. Shan,Komal,Ankita,He and I were together to play. Here we go and pen rolls and it comes to Komal she chose truth. I asked her, "How many times you have been kissed to his boyfriend?" She denied and said "I never kissed a boy". Again pen rolls and it came to Ankita she chose truth. I asked her to kiss Shan. Even she denied that she didn't kiss any boy. If I actually say my mind was being like, "fuck you". I mean really what the hell you doing why you telling lie if you kissed then what's wrong. But they never are going to accept that. Pen rolled and stopped at me I was asked for truth and dare. I chose dare and they told me to hug Shan. I was refused to do because there was someone whose heart was squeezing with this dare. But I did because I have to do. After so long it came to Digvijay he chose dare. It was I who am given him a dare to do to propose a girl who ever is going from outside the corridor. He did very smartly he found a girl who was passing through corridor. He stopped her and said, "I'm sorry but I have a dare to propose you". Again it came to him and it was a dare, to kiss me. The moment when it was asked to do I was shocked and smiling. My heart was beating super fast and he came closer I was on high sky. He touched his lips to my cheeks firstly right cheek and then on left cheek. I was completely overwhelmed and flushed. It was heart touching kiss. I was asked for my feeling of that kiss which kiss gave you intense feeling. I told them, "I have felt on my left cheek". I was so shy while expressing. Everyone was looking at me and I was flushing. After this we stopped the game I think we were done with the main topic of the day. Now we all had to go home because college is already dispersed. I and he left together and else those two girls gone with Shan. It was rain in winter and weather got chilled. We all reached home and took rest.

I have one more topic to share it was 11th of December and our colleges were going to close. He also had to go hometown we were discussing about celebrating New Year together. He had to go to his hometown and there is a lack of network. One day I messaged him but he didn't reply and from early morning I messaged him so many times. There was no reply and I have my attitude and I believe to maintain it. In the afternoon he did reply messaged me for all the messages and also apologize *for all late replies. I didn't reply because I don't want to let this late reply so easily. I wanted him to come to me and say sorry. But it doesn't happen and we spent 14 days like this. Checking phone all the time and doing no message.*

Today is 25th of December and 11:30 now. I did message him and greeted him with text, "Merry Christmas". Message not delivered and I didn't message again. It is 13:00 hours and his message came it was sorry for late reply here is network issue. We started message again but I have a belief of him that he will definitely call me to apologize. Yeah he did call and I couldn't pick it up and I called him back. He said I'm sorry blah blah conversations had. I remember I took that conversation into his anger again and he said, "I don't want to talk to you". For me it was his first time when he became so rude to me. I cut the call and the fight begins again. I switched off my phone first time. It was chilled winter I and my family was enjoying holy fire outside home with groundnuts. When I turned on my phone there were 5 missed calls of him. I called him back and there a voice came "TUMHARI MAA KI JAI ". I kept quiet and waited for his next word with the sigh of single breath. He said "HI" and I replied, "Yes". There he started convincing me politely. I actually convinced but I do not have show. He was trying to make me smile with his silly jokes. Meanwhile I heard a voice coming back from his side was, "Namaste Bhabhi g". I reacted and asked him "what is this?" He said cleverly, "my brother is so funny he calls Bhabhi to my female friends". I really got understand but I didn't mention that we both were smiling. He told me a joke was very funny so I recalled a joke as well.

I asked him to translate a sentence which was, "He gave me 14 and 15 rupees". He translated and laughed so long. This is so funny moment something went. After long conversation we cut the call to sleep tight in the night. And we have decided to meet again in the last day of month. As it was my first external exam on 31st of December so, I said meet me on that day.

Today is 31st of December and he and I are on his bike going college together. He asked me to hug him while he was driving. It was so long when he and I were together and I was feeling so good to see him together. I was sitting behind him with hugging him in the chilled winter in December. We reached college and went canteen to talk before my exam begins. We have complaint each other and felt relaxed. I hugged him for the first time. My hug was something like I hit my forehead with his forehead. And I told him our first hug with this type. My exam began and in the mean time he was spending his time with no one he had to wait for me for so long. I finished my exam and came back to him spent some time in canteen we moved then. We have decided to wish each other in the late night when 00:00 will come. He wanted me to wish him first New Year greetings. From 9:00 we have started conversation and it last till new year began.

Here it is guys this is 00:00 now and I wished everyone and him too. I called him and the voice came, “the number you are trying to call is busy”.

TO BE CONTINUED..............

Read rest of the story in next series "MY LOVEY DUBEY 2020 part-2 (a journey from you and me to us)"

Love Is A Great Feeling

Love is an emotion which take time to be expressed. Love is a feeling which moulds you in a good and positive way. When you are in love you feel special energy in you that keeps you strong and courageous. You start feeling everything around you. Love makes you sensible and strong. Love also finds out the real of you and takes it out to the world. You feel positivity around you. It happens like a miracle happened in your life. Love gives you the way to think positive and clear.

In this whole story Nisha and Digvijay who are different before meeting each other. Digvijay respected Nisha and gave her importance so, the perspective of her was changing. Love can change world it has power to change one's thought.

If you love someone do share your feeling . Do not wait for the right time to say just speak up. Might be another person is waiting for your expression.

Love Is A Great Feeling

Love is an emotion which needs to be expressed. Love is a feeling which moulds you in a good and positive way. [illegible]

Beginning Of Series 2

Oops pages end!

Don't worry, Author is here and she can read your mind. You want to know more about this love life. Here it does not ends with the end of the book pages. From now story begins with thier love . It was not possible to complete in a book so, i thought to take a pause I hope this pause will not distrube your reading.

Firstly so much thanks for reading this book. I believe you liked this book for you i'll update soon with the part -2 of "MY LOVEY DUBEY 2020". We will be meeting in the next part of this series. Cordially thanks to all those readers who brung their attention and precious time towards this book. Thanks for giving us this much love.

I can't tell you the whole story of next series but here i have a glance of that part.

(And we kissed today. We were supported by our environment there was no barrier no other person was there to distrub us for atleast 12 minutes.)

Keep in touch I'll write its 2nd part with the name "MY LOVEY DUBEY 2020 Part-2 " soon. Give lots love to this book .

9 798885 556378

Printed by Libri Plureos GmbH in Hamburg, Germany